5

Exeter

in old picture postcards volume 2

Peter Thomas

European Library ZALTBOMMEL/THE NETHERLANDS

Bibliography

Peter Thomas, author, local historian, photographer and lecturer, has been involved with the history of Exeter for over twenty-five years. Living and working in Exeter all his life he has gained a wide knowledge of the city and is an avid collector of images of Exeter. His private collection of archive photographs, called 'The Isca Historical Photographic Collection' is the largest private archive of its type and is recognized as being of local, regional and national interest and consists of around 60,000 images.

As an author and photographer, Peter Thomas has produced some of the most well-known Exeter Books, Old Exeter, Aspects of Exeter, A Century of Exeter, Exeter in old photographs, The changing face of Exeter, The House that moved, Exeter Yesterday and today and Fire on the Wind (The Exeter Blitz Illustrated). He has also produced a photographic book on Devon called 'Images of Devon' and a further publication called 'The Exe Estuary-Wildlife in Camera'. The Isca Collection has featured extensively in the press and the author has appeared on television and radio. Two commercial videos have also been produced: 'Old Exeter' and 'The Exeter Blitz'.

As a lecturer he has undertaken numerous talks to professional bodies, the University, local organizations and educational establishments. Audiences have exceeded 400 when undertaking special local history audio-visual presentations at the city's theatre.

In his former role as Tourism Promotion Officer for the City of Exeter he instigated a major tourism service 'Exeter Guided Tours' and used his personal knowledge to promote Exeter. He was the creator of the famous Exeter Redcoat Guides drawing 400,000 people into Exeter to undertake guided tours. In 1987 he was responsible for creating and managing the largest historical exhibition ever held in Exeter 'The Great Exeter Exhibition', attracting 10,000 people. Other initiatives have included 'The Exeter Historical Pageant' and 'The Exeter Medieval Fayre', the first ever to be held in the city.

Acknowledgements

To Mr. Don Lashbrook for the use of cards from his personal collection.
To Mrs. Lorna Till for checking of texts, general support, constant enthusiasm.

BACK IN TIME

European Library
post office box 49
NL – 5300 AA Zaltbommel/The Netherlands
telephone: 0031 418 513144
fax: 0031 418 515515
e-mail:publisher@eurobib.nl

Introduction

Exeter in old picture postcards volume 2 follows the printing of the first book in 1986 in which 140 postcard images of Exeter were published. The new volume adds to the resource showing a further 124 cards. The opportunity to produce these books has increased my own interest in the collecting of postcards enormously and I can now be classified as 'addicted' together with thousands of others who have taken up this fascinating pastime.

Cartology or postcard collecting is big business today with regular fairs and events that take place across the country. Whatever the personal interest, some one is specializing in it and as with all collecting the thrill of finding the rarity never goes away. For many people great interest is found in topographical cards that show views of cities, towns, villages and aspects of daily life. *Exeter in old postcards volume 2* will add, it is hoped, to the interest as to how Exeter has changed and looked in the past. It will relate to buildings and the general history of the city. Postcards can be roughly divided between massed produced printed cards, real photographic images and art cards, and all of interest for the local history collector. Certain postcard publishers have been knowned for the printed quality of their cards and this makes them more desirable. Real photographic images are the greatest treasure for the collector, as it is the photographic image that generally offers the rarest records of streets, events and daily life. The availability of printed photographic postcard paper allowed local photographers to produce images of their town or village and sometimes only a single image may have been produced, creating a rarity. In 1907 Postcard Gaslight Photographic Paper was being sold for 5/- for 100 sheets.

Exeter companies and photographic studios produced their own postcards and these included the Worth Art Gallery, Chandlers and the Cathedral Art Gallery. The greatest range of cards was produced by Worth's, who operated from Mols Coffee House in the Cathedral Close. The company took a particular interest in the history of Exeter and based much of their business on promoting historical aspects of Exeter and the region. Worth's produced their own Guide Book to Exeter in which they advertised their postcards:

POSTCARDS
WORTH'S UNIQUE SERIES
Set of 14 Brown tinted Mezzotint cards of Exeter 1/- set
Set of 14 Etching postcards B D Ward Quaint corners of Exeter 1/- set
Set of 6 Beautiful interior etchings Bradshaw Roper 1/- set

Set of 12 *Showing gates, sieges, receptions, historic personages 1/- set*
Set of 12 *Old ecclesiastical Exeter showing its oldest churches, Priory,*
Almshouses, Martyrs Relic.
Set of 6 *Old houses of Exeter watercolours TB Worth 1/- set*
Set of 12 *Devonshire Church screens*
Set of 12 *Church Screens*
Set of 12 *Old Devonshire Crosses*
Set of 12 *English Forts*
Set of 12 *Doorways*
Set of 16 *Misereres*
Set of 12 *Old Cornish Crosses*
Set of 12 *Devonshire thatched roofs*
Set of 12 *Romantic Exmoor*
Set of 12 *English Epitaphs*

National postcard publishers also featuring Exeter include Frith & Co, Valentine, Judges, Salmon, Welch of Portsmouth, Sweetman of Tunbridge Wells and J. Thridgould & Co of London who produced Milton Postcards called 'Gelatine View' with samples at 6 doz 2/- or 3/9 gross. Local publishers and photographers producing cards include Henry Wykes, Wheaton and Co, A. Eyres South Street, Southwoods, Amious R. Jerman 19 Sidwell Street, Stuart A. Moore, Fisher, South Street, Dawson and Sons Gandy Street, Charles Keeping, Cumming & Co 133 Fore Street, T. Fisher 37 South Street, Walter Scott, A.L. Brinicombe, J.L. Pitman 111 Fore Street, United Devon Association 17 Bedford Circus.

With the millions of postcards that have been sent since their inception it is unlikely that senders would have realized that their card could, one day, be a collectors item. The first postcard was sent in the USA in 1861 and had no picture, but in 1870 one of the first picture postcards bore an image of the Royal Polytechnic in Regent Street. Picture postcards were also produced in Germany and Switzerland in the same year. By the turn of the 19th century postcard sales were booming and the Golden Age of Postcards arrived between 1900 and 1918. With the First World War postcard production dwindled and did not revive until 1940. Although postcards are now part of the daily scene in modern life it is never likely to reach its former levels of interest.

The stopping of production of Postcard Photographic Paper purchased by local photographers also added to the decline of the more unusual postcard that today can be highly collectable.

For those who take an interest in their city, town, village or aspects of daily life the collecting of postcards is a valuable resource and reflects the changing of society over a period of 120 years.

Exeter, Peter Thomas

1　A view circa 1955 shows the full extent of the three hundred foot long lead-covered Cathedral roof supported by massive flying buttresses. Its length was only possible due to the construction of the two central towers being incorporated into the transcepts. The unbroken Gothic vaulted roof is the longest roof of its type in the world. The bomb blast screen is still seen protecting the Great East Window and Lady Chapel window. Shown above the North Tower are buildings that no longer exist in the Cathedral Close. The building set back was the Devon and Cornwall Bank opened in 1863. It was demolished together with adjacent buildings and the site rebuilt in the 1960s.

2   Exeter Cathedral is seen from the north-west and shows the West Front with its medieval image screen. The expanse of the Cathedral Close is seen left and was, until 1637, the city burial ground. Excavations have shown bodies buried in close proximity and one on top of the other. Skeletons have also been found outside of the grassed area, often when road works have taken place. The road passed right in front of the Cathedral with cars parked right up to the building.

EXETER.

3   Taken from the devastated area of South Street, through an existing standing brick arch, the boarded front of the Cathedral is shown with the remains of the bombed Vicars Choral Hall still standing. The Hall, part of what was once an extensive complex, was to be retained as a memorial to the Exeter Blitz of May 1942. South Street, a narrow thoroughfare before the war, was badly damaged by enemy bombing. The east side of the street totally collapsed after being targeted by high explosive bombs.

4   Exeter Cathedral is shown in the post-war period almost isolated, in an area cleared of all existing standing buildings. The view is taken from the original line of Paris Street. The remains of the Georgian Bedford Circus had been torn down and a huge area was to become a weed infested bombed site. A massive rebuilding programme was soon to give Exeter a completely new look.

5   An aerial view from the south shows Exeter Cathedral undergoing reconstruction after the last war. St. James' Chapel on the south side was completely destroyed leaving a huge hole in the side of the building. It was suggested that if a further flying buttress had been destroyed then the whole Cathedral roof could have collapsed. The chapel site is shown covered by a canopy allowing work to continue regardless of the weather. Cars are seen parked around the oval that was once part of Bedford Circus.

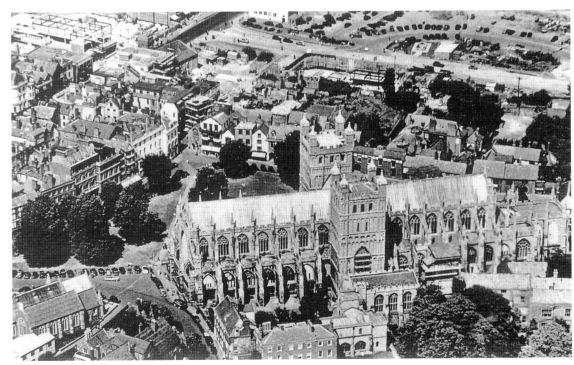

6   The Sidwell Street area is shown from the junction of York Road and Sidwell Street. Taken in the 1930s it shows, bottom left, the Acland Hotel that stood on the corner of Sidwell Street and York Road opposite the Duke of York pub. It is now 'All days Store'. The elaborate dome of the Methodist Church is clearly identified and today this decorative structure is illuminated. Sidwell Street was complete until 1936 when numbers 75 to 80 were to be removed for the building of the Odeon Cinema. Most buildings on the south side were destroyed in the Second World War. At the top of the photograph is shown St. James' Church, later blitzed, and the open space of St. James' Football Ground.

7   Some of Exeter's more unusual postcards are those that depict the results of the bombing of Exeter in May 1942. The cards were not mass produced but the work of individual photographers. Postcard Photographic Paper allowed the production of very limited numbers of cards or even a single image. Shown in this record are the gutted remains of Lloyds Bank in High Street with the partially removed Dellers Café above and to the side. St. Stephen's Church was saved and its famous chancel and bow narrowly escaped destruction. Part of High Street is shown already cleared.

8 The main façade of Lloyds Bank and Dellers Café that faced High Street and Bedford Street still stood after the bombing in May 1942. The imposing entrance with classical reclining figures leading into the café still graced Bedford Street. The substantially built structure proved more difficult to remove than had been anticipated and was to take several days to pull down. Dellers Café was a major focal point for social life in the city and it is curious that no effort was made to retain the structure or replace it.

9 Numerous buildings were to be destroyed by incendiary bombs around the area of the London Inn Square and East Gate. This postcard taken from the interior of a destroyed shop front looks towards the Savoy Cinema. Eighteen firebombs fell on the building but were ejected by courageous Fire Guards. The Plaza Cinema was engulfed by fire due to high explosives but its façade survived and is shown in this record. The remains were demolished.

10 The clearing of the central area of Exeter after the blitz of May 1942 was to take a number of days. Assistance was given by the military and over a period of days 5,000 men were drafted in to help clear the streets, remove unstable buildings and to look after the shocked population. The premises of Messrs. Bobby's in High Street, next to St. Stephen's Church, had been destroyed.

11   One of the most severely damaged streets in Exeter during the Second World War was Bedford Street. The Constitutional Club that stood on the corner of Catherine Street and Bedford Street was gutted. It had opened in 1884, but the ground floor was taken over in 1939 by Martins Bank, who altered the frontage. Public underground toilets, that were railed, existed in the middle of the street. With post-war redevelopment new toilets were constructed in Catherine Street.

12   Before the purchase of Rougemont Gardens by the City in the early twentieth century a grotto and fernery existed at the far north end of the Castle Moat. Another feature was a subterranean passage with a rustic gate that appeared to head right under the city wall towards Northernhay. On the other side of the wall stood Northernhay House, and the passage could have passed right under the building. The house was demolished before the Rougemont Gardens were opened to the public. There is no indication as to the use of the passage, but there is a possibility that it was not a passage but an ice house, a facility common to many fine houses in the 18th and 19th centuries. The photograph shows the city wall without the opening into Northernhay, this predates it to before 1913.

Exeter, Rougemont Castle, Subterranean Passage

13　The Exeter War Memorial in Northernhay Gardens is recognized as being one of the finest memorials in the country. The bronze statues are the work of the sculptor John Angel, who spent much of his early life in Exeter. He worked for the well-known Exeter company Wippell & Co, carving in wood and stone, and attended Lambeth School of Art and the Royal Academy of London. He was commissioned to undertake the Memorial that was unveiled on 24th July 1923. The central bronze is a statue of Liberty standing on a dragon. On each side of the four-sided plinth bronzes depict a prisoner of war, a soldier, a sailor and a nurse. Work is shown nearing completion with quantities of stone, pick axes and rope lying around the site.

14   On entering Northernhay Gardens from Northernhay Place the visitor is confronted by the bronze statue called 'The Deer Stalker,' the work of E.B. Stephens ARA. The statue was first exhibited in 1876 at the Royal Academy and priced at £1,000. Interest was expressed in keeping the work in Exeter and two committees set about raising money for its purchase. The artist, however, decided to gift the work to Exeter and it was first erected in Bedford Circus. It was unveiled in 1878 and attended by a huge public gathering, with speeches and a luncheon in honour of the sculptor in the New London Hotel. The Deer Stalker was moved to Northernhay Gardens and replaced in Bedford Circus by a bronze of William Reginald Courtenay Earl of Devon erected in 1880.

15 St. Nicholas' Priory, Exeter's oldest building, is shown from Mint Lane. Originally a Benedictine monastery only part of the complex exists. Founded in the 11th century the remaining former guest wing still retains its Norman Undercroft. The Priory continued until 1536 when under the Dissolution the Priory church and other parts of the building were demolished. The remaining two wings were sold by the Crown for conversion into Tudor houses.

16 In 1913, the City Council purchased St. Nicholas' Priory in a very dilapidated condition for the sum of £850. A major restoration programme was started with the intention of bringing the remaining structure back to its original appearance. Part of the project was to involve the removal of plaster from the Undercroft pillars exposing the ribs and fine Norman detail. A set of postcards was produced to promote the building.

17   The western front of St. Nicholas' Priory is shown before its restoration in 1913. Previously the façade had been clad with ivy, but at this point it had been stripped exposing details of changes to the structure over a period of time. Alterations had been made to its early windows with unsuitable additions. Work on the building reinstated features of appropriate monastic style and the doorway shown was changed to a large three-section bay window.

18   The first Curator of St. Nicholas' Priory, Miss Maude Tothill, is shown as a young woman standing outside the western front of the Priory, in what is now the garden. She stands beside the shaft of a Celtic cross that was placed there after being removed from 229 High Street, where it had acted as a cart buffer for 130 years. The shaft was acquired by William Nation, owner of the building, when the new Exe Bridge was constructed over the Exe in 1778. It may have been used for earlier bridge repairs or had some religious significance in relation to crossing the River Exe.

The Shaft of the 7th Cent. Preaching Cross,
around which probably the
Priory of St. Nicholas of Exeter grew.

19 Integrated into the Image Screen of the west front of Exeter Cathedral is a small chapel dedicated to Bishop Grandisson, who was responsible for re-building during the early and mid-14th century. The chapel, entered from a small door on the south side of the West Door, was constructed between the central and south porches. The arch, now filled in, allowed a view of Bishop Grandisson's tomb from the interior of the Cathedral. The tomb was ransacked during the Reformation (16th century) and the Bishop's remains cast out. Centuries later, during a cleaning programme the Bishop's gold ring was found. It bears an image of the Virgin and Child and today can be seen in the Cathedral Library.

20   Bishop Robert Mortimore (1949-1973) is seen on the Bishop's Throne or architectural throne canopy. A magnificent oak structure dating from 1313-1319 it is recognized as perhaps the finest and largest carved woodwork of its type in England and stands over 50ft high. It is constructed without the use of nails or screws and is securely fastened with oak pins. Prior to the Second World War the throne was dismantled and stored to avoid destruction. After the war it was completely reassembled to its original state.
The throne was built at a cost of £12-£14.

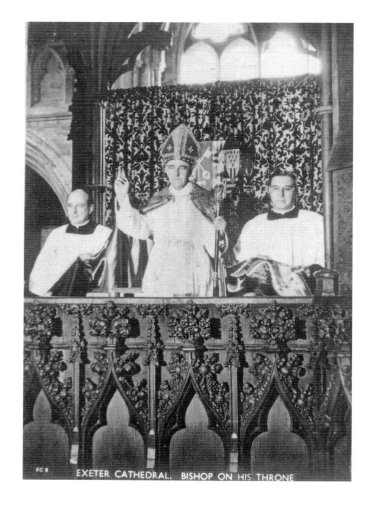

EXETER CATHEDRAL. BISHOP ON HIS THRONE

21 The Image Screen of Exeter Cathedral is one of the most important displays of medieval statuary in the country. Before the construction of the Image Screen the West Front consisted of three impressive doorways (1320-1340) but was to be faced with a remarkable three-tier structure bearing statues, the whole of which would have been highly painted creating a blaze of colour. Remnants of the paint can still be seen today. Exeter Cathedral has over the centuries been subject to pollution that has substantially affected much of the stonework. Over the last century the Dean and Chapter have instigated a number of conservation projects and in this record discoloration is clearly seen.

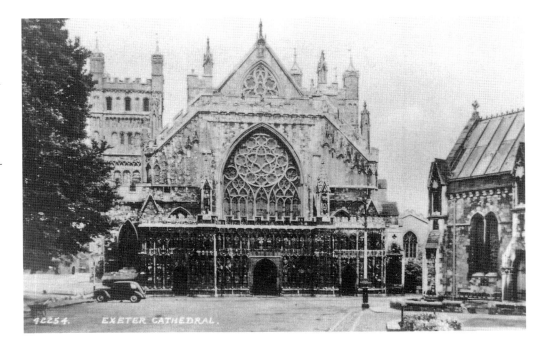

42254.   EXETER CATHEDRAL.

22 Exeter Cathedral was to undergo restoration in the early 19th century. In 1870 major work was undertaken under the direction of George Gilbert Scott, an eminent Victorian Gothic Architect. The project was completed in 1877. The Great East Window was restored in 1896. After the Second World War an appeal was set up to restore the war-damaged building and this was completed by 1961. The interior was cleaned between 1975 and 1982 and the West Front from 1968 to 1985. The start of cleaning the West Front is shown in this record.

23   The Chapter House, built circa 1225 under Bishop Brewer, was constructed for use by Canons and is shown as a library. The site was formerly part of the Bishop's Palace Garden. The wall niches shown left displayed medieval wall paintings but these were covered and fibreglass sculptures inserted in 1974. The Library was transferred from the Chapter House (shown) to the Bishop's Palace.

THE CHAPTER HOUSE.

24 The Deanery, lying in the shadow of the Cathedral, dates from the early 13th century but with many later additions. A prime feature is the Great Hall that was altered in the 18th century by inserting a Minstrels Gallery. Its late medieval, arched-braced Collar Roof is one of Exeter's finest. Remodelled on several occasions the Deanery is the largest of the Clergy Houses in the Cathedral Close and has been one of the most important venues for visiting Royalty and VIPs. A fine lead water tank is shown dating from 1707.

The Deanery showing Cathedral Towers. Exeter.
S.A.Chandler's Real Photo Series 04428.

25   Exeter's Cathedral Close is one of the finest in England surrounded by a number of buildings traditionally used by the Clergy. The east side of the Close contains a range of buildings that are architecturally and historically interesting and have the old world charms one expects of English towns. The six properties shown give an indication as to the age of buildings. St. Martin's Church (left) was consecrated in 1065, rebuilt in the 15th century and stands next to Mols Coffee House dating from around 1530. A substantial brick Georgian building, Number 5 The Close, was built in 1729. At the rear is a much earlier and exciting building, the Hall of the Annuellars College dating from 1529. The Annuellars College extended from Number 5 Cathedral Close to Mols Coffee House, but following the demolition of the front section of the College the buildings shown were constructed.

CATHEDRAL CLOSE SHOWING MOL'S COFFEE HOUSE, EXETER

26 A charming record looking down the east side of the Close gives a much more enclosed feel to the area than one gets today. The Close was railed at this time and Numbers 5 and 6 are covered in creepers and also have their original railings. These were to disappear from Exeter, as part of the war effort and in most cases never replaced. Number 7 The Close, the Devon and Exeter Institution is shown with its frontage rendered. This was later removed exposing its Heavitree stone construction. The property was originally the town house of the Courtenay family, the Earls of Devon, but converted into a library in 1814.

CATHEDRAL CLOSE. EXETER. No.104.

27 The north-east corner of the Cathedral Close has always been an attraction for visitors. The combination of the Royal Clarence Hotel, St. Martin's Church, Mols Coffee House and adjoining 18th-century buildings present a very pleasing townscape. It has been a hot spot for photographers and is probably the most photographed part of the city. The earliest known photographic record of Exeter was taken outside Mols dated about 1860.

28 Taken a short distance from the Globe Hotel this view shows the north aspect of the Close. The railings enclose the site where the County Memorial, designed by Sir Edwin Lutyens, was placed in 1921. On the left is shown the Cathedral Restaurant and adjacent to it the railed frontage of the Devon County Bank built in 1836. Its neighbour Wippell & Co had their premises purpose-built in 1883 on the site of houses previously destroyed by fire. The new premises in Victorian Gothic style stretched from the Close to High Street and were numbered 55 & 56 High Street. Wippell's still operate in Exeter and continue to supply church furniture and clerical outfits, having an international reputation. The company left Cathedral Close in 1983 and now operate from St. Thomas.

Cathedral Close, Exeter.

29　A drawing from a postcard series published by Worth's of Exeter illustrates the passageway leading to the Law Library at Number 8 The Close. The view looks toward the Cathedral. It clearly shows the system for security relating to important medieval buildings. Large properties in the Close were set back and protected by Gate Houses incorporating enormous wooden doors. A connecting corridor above the main door allowed any caller to be viewed before entry.

A PEEP OF THE CLOSE. EXETER.　WORTHS SERIES

30   It is difficult to imagine this scene today of West Street and Stepcote Hill as the major road system Western Way has transformed the area.
To the left is seen the entry to Frog Street. The Teignmouth Inn, shown right, was removed in 1961. Just past the public house is the corner of Ewings Lane and the entry to Cricklepit Street.

WEST GATE & STEPCOTE HILL, EXETER   WORTHS SERIES

31 Paul Street today is an ugly service road and bears no resemblance to the drawing shown here. The Street had numerous older buildings that extended up its northern side, but by the turn of the twentieth century these had mostly been removed. The large open site was to have a new purpose. It was transformed into the City's Coach and Bus Station. Buses left from the higher level and coaches from the lower. The station moved in 1964 to Paris Street and in the mid-1980s the site was transformed into the Harlequin Shopping Centre. The drawing shows the front of St. Paul's Church left removed in 1936.

PAUL STREET. EXETER.

32 St. Stephen's Church in High Street is a survivor from the last war and is one of the few churches left in the city centre. The origins of the church are 11th-century but its exterior mid-17th-century. Beneath the church is an ancient sealed Saxon crypt that is supported by short Norman columns. The crypt was discovered in 1826 but later sealed with no access possible today. Whilst buildings were destroyed around the church in the Second World War St. Stephen's sustained little damage except to its chancel. The tenacity of the Fire Guards saved the church.

ST STEPHENS CHURCH. EXETER.   WORTH'S SERIES.

33 The famous Bow of St. Stephen's Church is seen looking from Stephen Street into High Street. The chancel, which is supported by the Bow, was divided from the main body of the church in 1972. The drawing shown, executed under the name of C. Russell, is a false name used by John Shapland, artist of Exeter, whose business, the Cathedral Art Gallery, operated from Number 1 Catherine Street (SPCK).

34 The ancient town house of the Poltimore's is from the Worth's Series of Postcards. The building was more commonly known as Bampfylde House, a substantial Heavitree stone mansion that stood on the corner of Catherine Street and Bampfylde Street. Started by Richard Bampfylde in 1590 the building was completed by his son Amias. The property remained with the Bampfylde's until after the First World War, when it was sold to private owners. Latterly the property was bought by the City for £5,000 and opened as a museum in 1934 when, for the first time, the public could view its fine interior. This wonderful property was unfortunately totally destroyed in the last war.

WORTHS SERIES. EXETER. ANCIENT TOWN HOUSE OF THE POLTIMORES.

35   A postcard sent on 9th October 1904 by Jeanette Rowe depicts 'The Quadrangle' at Number 10 Cathedral Close as seen from the inner archway. Beyond the arch the visitor sees a delightful group of early ecclesiastical buildings. Originally the residence of the Archdeacon of Barnstaple the property was altered in the 17th century. A tiny chapel is incorporated in the building and seen in the centre of the drawing. A humorous addition is the chicken eating in the archway.

The Quadrangle EXETER.

Oct 9th 1904
Jeannette Rowe.

36　Some of the most evocative historical illustrations are those undertaken by S. Endacott. A range of historical paintings were produced that have the atmosphere of past times. The illustration shown is Number 45 High Street and one of the city's oldest buildings, now occupied by Thornton's the chocolate makers. The narrow three-storeyed building dates from about 1550 with a cellar and steps leading up to the street. The carved timber frame building oversails the High Street, a typical feature of its period.

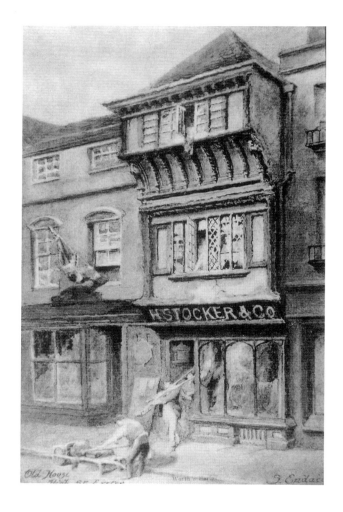

37   In Catherine Street today, the Heavitree stone ruins of St. Catherine's Almshouses have been landscaped as a public rest area. The site has been retained as a memorial to the Exeter Blitz of 1942. The Almshouses, founded in 1450 by Canon Stevens, were maintained to house thirteen poor men. A shell of the small chapel still stands complete with its bell turret and single bell.

22 EXETER. — Old Alms Houses, Catherine Street.

38 In central Fore Street, on the north side, a late-19th-century frontage hides a remarkable interior from the late-15th century. It is Tuckers Hall, formerly a chapel and meeting place of the Guild of Weavers, Fullers and Shearmen. Its atmosphere is unique in the city. Converted from a chapel to a hall with the addition of an extra floor after the Reformation, it is still the home of Exeter's most ancient Guild.

Rich wooden carved wall panels were added between 1634 and 1638 and in the 20th century a wonderful wagon roof was uncovered.

39 At the junction of Smythen Street and King Street stood before the war a very ancient building known as the Norman House, but little was known of its history. In the 1920s it was almost derelict, but part of a Norman doorway was found and investigations suggested that it was possibly a twelfth-century building that had been altered in the 15th century. It had also been divided into two dwellings. A plaster ceiling had been taken down but still remained. The building had a collar braced roof and Norman friezes still existed on the walls. All the indications suggested that some noteworthy person had at one time owned the building. The building was restored but destroyed in 1942.

Old House, King Street.   Worth's Series.

40 The River Exe is shown towards Blackaller Weir, Mount Dinham and St. Michael's and All Angels' Church. The river retains a rural feel with natural banks. The cliffs of Mount Dinham dominate with the 220 feet spire of St. Michael's Church overseeing the whole area. The church, built in 1865, has the highest spire of any church in Exeter. Below at the rivers edge is seen the now demolished chimney of Head Weir Mill. To the far right are timber drying sheds used by Webbers Timber Merchants. The structure was destroyed by fire at a later date.

41 A good view is recorded looking from the west bank of the Exe across the new single span Exe Bridge that opened in 1905. From the late 18th century buildings were constructed to lead right up to the three-arched bridge that was completed in 1778 and these were retained up to the late-20th century. The townscape provided an attractive entry into the city. In modern times this element has been mostly lost. This record shows left the Crown Co Photographers, operating from a daylight studio overlooking the River Exe. They also specialized in frame making, carving and gilding. Advertised centrally are A.E. Mogg Cash Drapers and Milliners and far right are the City Brewery and tower of St. Edmund's Church.

The Exe Bridge, Exeter.

42 Taken from Shooting Marsh Stile this rare view looking towards Exe Bridge captures citizens enjoying an unusual opportunity, walking and skating on the frozen river. To the right of the bridge at the beginning of Commercial Road a flight of wooden steps lead down to the river giving access to leisure boats. Dozens of people crowd on to Exe Bridge to watch the spectacle.

43 Leisure boats were a common sight on the River Exe giving endless hours of pleasure to many Exeter people. Vessels could be hired from the Quay, Exe Bridge and the Seven Stars Hotel, who invested in a floating platform. On the opposite side of the river at the back of the livestock market a company called 'Dorothys' operated hire boats at the turn of the 20th century.

44　A pair of flood-gates known as Kings Arms Sluice control the entry of water into the canal. They are closed when the Exe is in flood to prevent damage to the canal banks. A Royal coat of arms once stood on a site near the gates. The sluice enabled light shipping to reach the quayside across the river to discharge and load cargoes. The sluice keeper's cottage can be seen left.

45   In an age of modern facilities it may come as a surprise that the river was used for swimming pursuits. The city created changing facilities and diving platforms at Head Wear. Operated by the City Council an attendant was on site at all times to ensure the safety of swimmers.

46 A scarce record shows the Custom House on Exeter Quay. It is recognized as the earliest surviving brick building in the city being constructed in 1681. H.M. Customs undertook their duties from this building for 308 years before leaving in 1989. The original design included open arcading to allow goods to be brought in under cover, but this feature was in filled at a later date. The bay of the Custom House, shown right, was brought forward to create an additional office for the Customs Officers. A substantial internal staircase leads to the Long Room on the first floor that is adorned with one of the finest plaster ceilings in Devon, the work of John Abbot of Frithelstock, North Devon. Ships captains presented their papers in the Long Room. This photographic record of the Custom House may be one of the earliest dating from 1913. A dwarf wall exists in the front of the building, which is railed and partially covered with ivy.

Custom House, The Quay, Exeter.

S.A. Chandlers
Real Photo Series.
02888

47 Haven Banks takes its name from the creation of a 'safe haven' for vessels. Before the building of the Basin the area had a natural depression shown as being water filled on early maps. It had the necessary features for the creation of a floating harbour and was to be the last stage of completion for the Exeter Ship Canal. A ferry service has traditionally run from Haven Banks to the Quay since 1641. The service is today operated by the use of a hand wire crossing the Exe.

THE QUAY. AND FERRY. EXETER.

SS47

48 Taken at the turn of the 20th century this image records Exeter Quay as it will never be seen again. Within seventy years of this photo all commercial shipping had stopped. On the right is seen St. Leonard's Quay piled high with scrap iron that was used for ballast in departing ships. All buildings at this end of the Quay have been removed and new housing built in the last ten years.

49   On entering the Exeter Ship Canal vessels were required to be towed by teams of horses. There were various stopping places and stables along the 5¼ mile length of the Canal. The waterway had towing paths for horses that worked from both sides. This is recorded in this image. This scarce photograph is taken at Seages Swing Bridge, now removed. It was on the bend of the Canal just before Salmon Pool Bridge. Crossing the bridge you entered land belonging to Bonham's Farm. Three horses are shown with two pulling on the far bank and a single animal, left, with its handler.

50 Previously to the current bridge at Countess Wear a wooden structure was operated by hand under the control of a bridge keeper. The keeper's cottage stood beside the bridge and was known as Drawbridge Cottage. In the early 20th century Countess Wear Swing Bridge was operated by Hannah Shoreland and it was an unusual occupation for a woman. Up to 296 vessels passed safely up the Canal under Hannah's guidance. In the Second World War preparations for D Day landings took place at the swing bridge and Hannah was sworn to secrecy about the activities. Her latter years were spent beside the Canal (with her cat) ensuring her bridge was immaculately kept.

CANAL AT COUNTESS WEIR EXETER

51 An incident occurred at Countess Wear Swing Bridge in 1934 when a coaster filled with 300 tons of coal became stuck and part of the vessel had to be cut away to allow it to pass to the Exeter Basin. The event caused a huge traffic problem and a decision was then made to change the narrow bridge and electrify it. A steel bridge 107ft long, 20ft wide with a five feet pathway was commissioned by Devon County Council. It was opened on 2nd March 1937. It is a counterpoise bridge rising upwards and sideways, operated from a special control box on the Countess Wear side.

52   The Canal Basin or 'floating harbour' completed the construction of the Exeter Ship Canal. The new facility, 917ft long, 110ft wide and 18ft deep, allowed a number of vessels to offload goods without having to navigate across the River Exe to the Quay. On 29th September 1830 the Basin was opened with over 13,000 people joining in the celebration. It was to be linked to the main railway line with tracks being laid directly to the Basin's edge. Both broad and narrow gauge lines were used and linked to turntables allowing trucks to pass down the Basin to waiting ships.

The Basin, Exeter.

53 At its peak the Exeter Ship Canal was being visited by up to 300 vessels a year with a wide variety of goods being imported and exported. A fine record shows two vessels about to leave the Basin and enter the Canal. The tall chimney was part of the electricity generating station, built 1905.

54 This particular record is a wonderful example of the rural nature of Exeter in the early part of the 20th century. A shepherd has driven his flock of sheep over the narrow stone-built Countess Wear Bridge and passes the Toll House. The property was compulsorily purchased and demolished in January 1983. In latter years it had operated as a shop. The widening of the road from two to four lanes sealed the fate of the building. A farmer with his horse and cart follows the shepherd.

55 Mols Coffee House, in the Cathedral Close, was occupied by Worth & Co Art Gallery, from 1885 to 1965. Worth's produced a range of postcards of Exeter, of which this is one. The building is shown before its elaborate Dutch style gable was added in the 1870s. The reason for the addition of the feature is unknown, but it was to make the building into one of the most photographed in the city.

21 EXETER. — Mol's Coffee House in 1800. Now Worth's Art Gallery.
Worth's Series

56 The first floor panelled room of Mols Coffee House has traditionally been referred to as 'The Oak Room', the panels display forty-six carved coats of arms relating to well-known Devon families. The rare star-shaped ceiling has slots integrated into its design that allowed Worth's to lower huge gilded picture frames from the workshop above to the lower floors. The narrow winding staircase made movement throughout the floors a major problem.

57 The 12th-century St. Pancras' Church is shown before its restoration in the 1880s. In the 1930s the little church, one of the oldest in the city, was threatened with removal due to impending redevelopment. The church was retained by agreement and some demolition took place around the building. In the 1970s the whole area was decimated for the construction of the Guildhall Shopping Centre that was called 'The Golden Heart Project'. The little building survived, but surrounded by bland architecture. The 15th-century church bell still remains and bears an inscription 'I am small but I am well heard over a wide area'.

57 EXETER. — St. Pancras Church before Restoration.

58   The church of St. Petrock in High Street has origins going back to the twelfth century. It has been greatly altered and enlarged. The interior is confusing, as the original chancel, that faced eastwards, was replaced in 1881 by a new chancel that faced southwards. The high street frontage was also opened up in 1905 after the removal of buildings that abutted upon the church. In the 1990s a major change took place when most of the building was transformed into a centre for the homeless. The facility was operating by early 1995 and today only the original chancel area is open to the public.

59 A commemorative postcard was produced for the opening of St. Sidwell's Methodist Church on 3rd May 1905. The ornate building with its octagonal dome (now illuminated at night) was constructed by the use of reinforced brickwork, a completely new concept for the time and the innovation of Paul Cotticin. Two open horse-drawn carriages wait outside.

Photo by F. Chorley.

St. Sidwell's Wesleyan Church, Exeter.
Opened May 3rd, 1905.

60 The exterior of St. Petrock's is shown after the High Street clearance of crowded old dwellings built against the church. This was done to widen the street for the arrival of the new electric trams service in 1905. For the first time in two centuries the arches of the original (now blocked) lower windows were revealed. The upper windows had been added to allow light to penetrate the gloomy interior of the church.

Exeter, St. Petrox Church.

61   A very rare view shows Southernhay Congregational Church as seen from Southernhay East. This road no longer exists in its original form. The top end of Southernhay can be seen right with a lady passing by. The street led directly from the London Inn Square into Southernhay and was lined with some fine buildings. The street was destroyed in the Blitz of May 1942.

62 A view looking up Southernhay East from the entrance of Dix's Field, right shows one of Exeter's least recorded streets. The street led to the London Inn Square.

63   Southernhay Congregational Church is recorded from the north side of Southernhay looking across the central gardens and shows the west end of the church. The site had previously been public baths, but these were demolished and a new church was built in 1868. The prominent Victorian church was badly bombed in May 1942 and gutted. Miraculously its tower survived and a new building created around it in the post-war period.

Southernhay Congregational Church, Exeter

64 St. Edmund's Church is today a ruin, retained as part of a landscaped area surrounding Exeter's medieval Exe Bridge. From the earliest times a church had been associated with the ancient bridge, but the first one was lost to fire in 1832. It was replaced in 1833. The interior of the early-19th-century church is not often seen.

St. Edmunds Church, Exeter.

—04892.

Chandlers Exeter Series.

65 Before the war, no one visiting Exeter was likely to miss the Church of St. Lawrence in central High Street. It stood where the Cooperative Bank is situated today. The building dating mainly from the 15th century was railed across its frontage. Entry to the church was through a porch constructed in 1694 from stone taken from the demolished conduit situated in High Street. A figure of Elizabeth 1, that had adorned the conduit, was integrated into the porch. The statue survived the last war and can be seen at the underground passages reception area at Roman Gate in High Street.

66 St. Lawrence Church in High Street contained a number of wall tablets and floor slabs bearing inscriptions of those buried beneath and a small churchyard existed at the rear of the church. Entry to the burial ground was by a small side passage from High Street. A gallery crossed the west end of the church and the cradle roof was decorated with gilded bosses, faces, knots and foliage. Elaborate 15th-century carved stalls divided the church and a feature of the interior was a regalia rack, used to hold the City Regalia when the Mayoralty attended services in state.

St. Lawrence Church, Exeter.

67   The small medieval church of St. Martin completes an attractive townscape in the north-east corner of the Cathedral Close. The first church on the site was dedicated in 1065. In 1995 services ceased as the congregation had dwindled to nine, but the building has remained open to the public.

This postcard shows the church interior during the early 20th century in poor condition. But the building has since been well restored and has been listed as one of the top 50 churches in England by The Churches Conservation Trust.

68   On 13th October 1886 a new theatre opened in Exeter at the junction of New North Road and Longbrook Street. It replaced the previous Bedford Street theatre that had been destroyed by fire. The new building accommodated 1,453 persons with prices for seats ranging from 5/- for the dress circle to 6p for the gallery. The theatre site was also constructed with shops at the ground floor level on the Longbrook Street side with dressing rooms above. Shown to the left in the postcard is a cabbies box offering transport to and from the theatre. It is adjacent to the stables of the New London Hotel.

69 One of the worst events in Exeter's history was to occur at the Theatre Royal on 5th September 1887. The tragedy was recorded by Exeter photographer Charles Keeping. During the performance of Romany Rye, which was playing to a full house, a huge fire engulfed the stage causing enormous panic from the audience. The poor design of exits resulted in passageways quickly jamming with people causing a horrendous situation. Trapped inside the theatre 186 people died from asphyxiation and then were burnt. The tragedy instigated the introduction of the safety fire curtain into every English theatre.

70   One of the most popular events at the Theatre Royal was the annual Christmas Pantomine that was attended by hundreds of Exeter children. Here is a piece of stage magic as Cinderella's coach is drawn on stage by four white ponies.

· Cinderella's Fairy Coach ·

71　The impressive entrance to the East Gate Arcade is shown in this record from the Chandler Real Photo Cards. Chandlers, the photographers, had an impressive studio in the arcade and produced a series of postcards of Exeter, recording some of the city's interesting aspects. Created by the Exeter Coffee Tavern Company in 1881 the Arcade was to be a popular shopping venue featuring twenty-two shops.

72   Exeter's East Gate Arcade was designed to allow the maximum quantity of daylight to be used by the construction of a glass covered roof for the whole of its length. At its south end a huge round stained glass window faced the shoppers as they entered the Arcade. Decorative iron gates kept the premises secure at night and controlled by a security officer seen standing in the middle of the arcade. Some of the city's most prestigious businesses including milliners, lace shops, umbrella makers, photographers, jewellers, gift shops and chemists operated from the building. The East Gate Arcade was destroyed by fire in the blitz of 4th May 1942.

73   Maynard's Girls' School, originally called 'The High School for Girls' stands at the junction of Denmark Road and Barnfield Hill. The substantial building, constructed in 1887, featured a large number of classrooms, laboratory and facilities for teaching cooking. Scholars numbered around 160 and the premises could be visited on presenting a visiting card. The school was founded in 1658 by Sir John Maynard, legal advisor to William III. The High School for Girls was aimed at attracting young ladies connected with the elite of the neighbourhood and daughters of Army and Navy Officers living in Devon.

74 Two of Exeter's most historic buildings are shown with a tram traction pole outside. The buildings were to be integrated and opened as the Chevalier Inn in 1940. The right-hand one, number 79 Fore Street, displayed a famous equestrian statue on its roof and at this time is occupied by J.A. Martin Booksellers. Even well into the 20th century the premises only had gas lighting on the first floor, no bathroom, a small sink with cold water and an outside toilet. One of Exeter's first tourist guides of Exeter's underground passages, Mr. Percy Martin, lived here. The buildings were tragically lost in the blitz of May 1942. Adjacent to Number 78 Fore Street was Lloyds Cigarette Factory and displayed is the sign for Eastman the Butchers on the corner of South Street.

75 The Mayor's Parlour at Exeter Guildhall is on the first floor of the Elizabethan portico that straddles the pavement in High Street. It is the official address of the Mayor and the room where dignitaries, VIPs and guests are welcomed. It was first used as a Council Chamber in 1594. The Mayor's Parlour was designed in 1900 after an extensive restoration of the portico and front of the Guildhall that was undertaken by Mr. Herbert Read. The oval plaster ceiling was removed in the 1990s and renewed due to structural defects. A main feature of the room is the large carved table, the work of Exeter ecclesiastical sculptor Harry Hems.

76 The Rougemont Hotel was built to service the new railway that had entered Queen Street in 1860 and operated from 1st February 1862. The hotel was completed in 1879 at a cost of £30,000 and had been built on the site of the old City Prison. It is shown with its original railings and entrance pillars. A half round landscaped railed garden existed opposite the hotel but was removed when the station was rebuilt in 1933.

49   EXETER. — Rougemont Hotel. — LL.

77 This view taken from new North Road looks towards the Miles Memorial Clock Tower. On the right is the entrance to Veitch Nurseries, opened in 1864 by Robert Veitch, one of the world famous family of horticulturalists and plant collectors. The company also opened a seed shop in High Street but later transferred to Number 17 Cathedral Close. In 1931 the Nurseries in New North Road closed and transferred to Alphington. The business was sold in 1969.

St. Davids Church and Clock Tower, Exeter.

78 This detailed photograph shows the interior of the Vicars Choral Hall in South Street, where the blitzed ruins can be seen today. The building was altered in the 16th century and fine panelling installed. The stone fireplace was carved with the crests of past bishops and a section still remains in St. Nicholas' Priory in Exeter. The central chair, known as 'The Custos Chair' and now in the Deanery, was said to reflect the style of Charles I, with its carved back panel of possible Dutch or Flemish origin. The Vicars Choral of the Choir of the Cathedral Church of St. Peter was formerly disbanded in 1933 and the Hall was blitzed in May 1942.

Fire Place, College Hall, Exeter.

79   William Mackworth Praed, a banker, obtained a site in the Cathedral Close and in 1769 opened what was to be the first hotel in England. The site also incorporated a bank built adjacent to the hotel. This postcard shows that the Exeter Bank had vacated the premises that were occupied by Dellers Café. The company opened in 1906. The successful business expanded and opened new purpose-built premises in 1916 on the corner of Bedford Street and High Street and became the centre of social life in Exeter. The hotel now incorporates what was the Exeter Bank building.

Exeter, Clarence Hotel and Dellers Cafe

80　The Royal Clarence Hotel is shown with a false canopy secured by large hooks incorporated into the façade. It covered the original portico. During recent years the canopy has been removed following hotel refurbishment and the building is now seen as it was first built. The portico is shown bearing the name of 'Stanbury' on its facia, reflecting the owner of the time and the coat of arms of the Duchess of Clarence.

81   Two 17th-century buildings, numbers 16 and 17 The Close are shown next to the Royal Clarence Hotel. Number 16 is clearly signed 'St. Martin's on the Well' and invites inspection and at this time is under the ownership of J. Commin Bookseller. Evidence suggested the two buildings were once one with site origins going back to the Norman period. Major alterations took place in the 15th century and excavations in the 1930s discovered a deep well and a substantial tunnel. Relics were also found. The proprietors took full advantage and promoted the building making it a new attraction for Exeter. Number 17 is shown occupied by Veitch, who used the premises for the selling of seeds.

82 Heavitree stone steps lead down to the cellar of the Well House, but a more interesting feature attracts attention today, a skeleton is entombed in the wall behind glass. A notice states 'Birth is the first step to death'! The cellar can be visited.

83 Number 1 Catherine Street is shown as the Cathedral Art Gallery and under the ownership of the artist John Shapland. The property was used as an outlet for his work. A prolific artist Shapland produced a large number of paintings relating to England, Scotland and Wales that were reproduced as postcards. The range was extensive and the images hand tinted. The cards were referred to as 'Brunotypes'. The work of hand tinting was carried out as a family business. John Shapland acted as the Headmaster for Exeter College of Art in his early years and had a studio in his house in Topsham Road, Exeter.

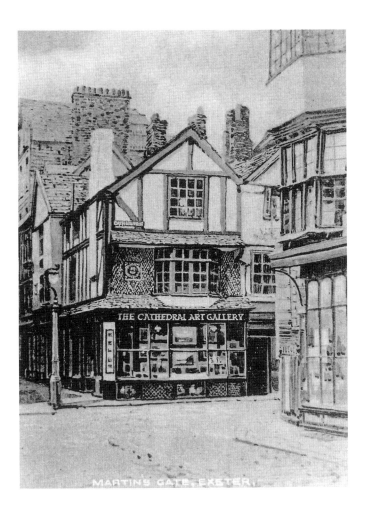

84 The pre-war Cathedral School was situated at the south-east end of the Cathedral Close and stood behind Numbers 11 and 12 The Close. It backed on to Bedford Circus that can just be seen left. The building was first designed as a Diocesan Training College and latterly used as the Cathedral School for training Choir Boys until the Second World War. A Headmaster ran the school and grants were given to deserving pupils. The building was mostly destroyed in 1942.

Cathedral School, Exeter.
The School House.

85   To further the needs for art, science and literature a University College was built at the rear of the Royal Albert Memorial Museum. Work commenced in 1911 after the purchase of houses and gardens. The site was called Bradninch Place. A training College was built at a cost of £24,500. It is now the Phoenix Art Centre. The building is shown with its original gates. As with many buildings in Exeter iron railings were removed to help with the war effort during the Second World War.

86 The West of England Eye Infirmary, now the Hotel Barcelona, was constructed between 1898 and 1901 at a cost of £25,000. The building was designed to accommodate 85 beds plus outpatients. After 91 years the facility closed and transferred to the main hospital site at Wonford. The site of the Eye Infirmary was formerly a large house that was demolished.

Exeter, West of England Eye Infirmary.

87 On 8th September 1915 King George V and Queen Mary came to Exeter to visit the war wounded accommodated at the West of England Eye Infirmary and the Memorial College Hostel in Gandy Street. At the Eye Infirmary all wards were visited and also the gardens, where a large number of recovering soldiers met the royal couple. King George was the first monarch to visit Exeter for 127 years.

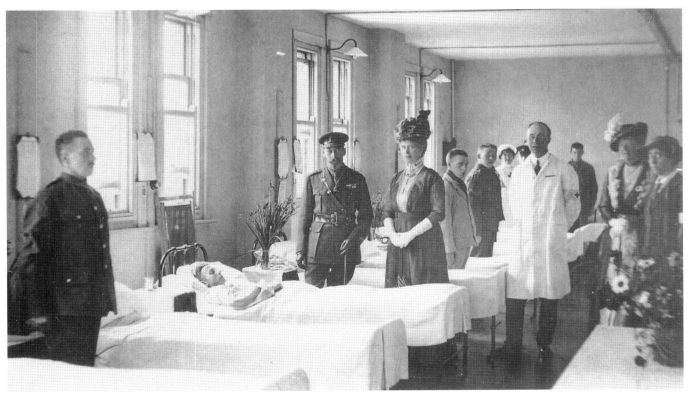

88 The famous building Dellers Café, opened in 1916, is shown from Bedford Street. Its impressive ornate arched entrance with classical reclining figures is shown to the left. Following the demolition of the Half Moon Hotel, Lloyd's Bank had built a single-storeyed building on the site. Dellers, a Paignton based company, constructed their premises above and to the side of the building, extending along Bedford Street. The business became a huge success and the focal point for social life in Exeter. The café was severely gutted during the last war but the substantial structure still stood, but was later demolished. The photograph shows the railed underground toilets situated in the middle of the street.

89   The stylish interior of Dellers glass roofed tiered restaurant was constructed with two large balconies embellished with plaster relief and supported by Corinthian columns. Discrete curtained alcoves allowed romantic private dining. A piano and music stand is shown and orchestras, bands and singers provided entertainment.

90 Dellers Café could undertake catering for very large parties and the kitchen boasted the most up-to-date facilities including the latest form of dishwasher.

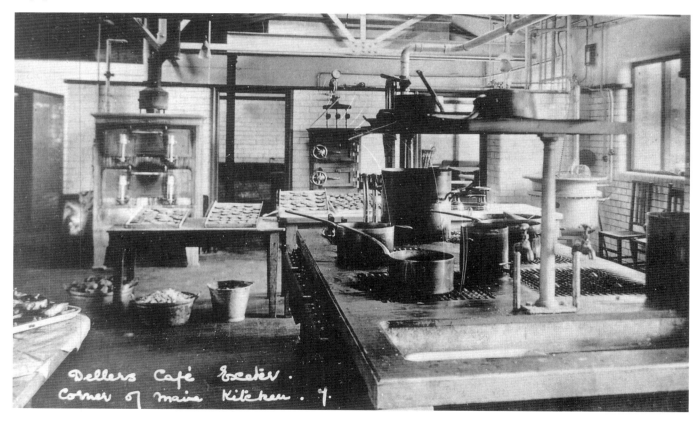

Dellers Café Exeter.
Corner of main kitchen. y.

91 The Palace Gate Convent School closed in 1997 and the premises were converted into private residences. Originally built in the 13th century for the Archdeacon of Exeter, the house was purchased in 1896 for the teaching order of French nuns known as 'The Institute of the Presentation of Mary' and the only establishment of their community in the country. The house was partly rebuilt and adapted as a girls' school. Further extensions were added in the 1920s. The recent conversion revealed a huge wooden cruck beam supporting the roof of the main stone building.

The Convent. Palace Gate. Exeter. Entrance.

92   This interesting promotional postcard shows the 3d and 6d stores of F. W. Woolworth & Co at Numbers 191 and 192 High Street. The site had been completely rebuilt for the company in 1934 and had previously been the extensive double fronted shop of Garton and King Ironmongers, who had occupied number 191 High Street. Its neighbour Pinder and Tuckwell traded from 192 High Street. Today the premises are operated by Mc. Donald's.

WOOLWORTH'S PREMISES, EXETER,
MONKS PARK STONEWORK
SUPPLIED AND FIXED BY
THE BATH & PORTLAND STONE FIRMS Ltd.

93 The wholesale iron-mongers Newcombe & Co traded from a large building at 109 Fore Street, the site of today's arcade. This postcard was used as a calling card. The property was referred to as 'The Old Star' Iron Stores and included twenty-two show-rooms extending from Fore Street to Smythen Street. All aspects of iron-mongery was sold together with lamps and oil. Another speciality was the supply of coffins and coffin furniture. Engraved breastplates could be produced at the shortest notice!

94 The front of St. David's Station is shown around 1910 with a tram stopping to pick up passengers. A horse-drawn parcel carrier waits patiently. A simple station was built in 1844 and this was improved in 1864. In 1910-1912 a major construction and extension project created the building shown. The whole frontage of the building was finished with decorative stone finials, which have now been removed. The front area of the station is shown as an enclosed grassed area and is now a car park.

95   The premises of the Cathedral Dairy stood at East Gate facing the London Inn Square and at the time shown under the ownership of the Exeter Cooperative Society. In the 1890s the company received milk from within an area of 30 miles and turned it into cream, butter and junket. Special separators used on the first floor worked at a speed of 6,500 revolutions per minute and separated milk was sold for 3d a gallon. It was described as a 'cheap boon for the poorer classes'. A special cooling room for cream used large quantities of steam pans and junkets were made to order. Devon honey, bottled fruits and other retail goods were sold.

96 Rougemont Castle was built on the highest point in the city, by the Normans in 1068 and was an ideal defensive position.

A group of buildings were later constructed inside the enclosure and a Sessions House in 1618. In 1774 the building was removed and replaced by new Crown Courts. It is now being considered that, after 227 years, the Crown Courts should be moved elsewhere due the lack of space and inadequate facilities. A covered wagon is seen leaving the courtyard.

97　A view taken from the Guildhall portico shows the Heavitree and Pinhoe tram filled with passengers and proceeding up High Street. The shop blind of 'Knapmans' the drapers is seen left on the corner of Goldsmith Street and on the far right the premises of 'The City Ironmongery Store'. Next door is 'The Devon and Cornwall Bank' whose main façade was in the Cathedral Close.

98   A view taken just beyond Bedford Street shows, left, the rounded dome of Dellers Café and on the right the Devon and Somerset Stores displaying its prominent blind. Next door, ironmongers Wippell Bros & Row, established in the late 18th century, had a partially timbered frontage. They were one of Exeter's oldest trading companies. The four-storeyed building had showrooms on the ground and first floors and at the rear of the building a manufactury. Wippells employed whitesmiths, locksmiths, bell hangers, and gasfitters and undertook all aspects of the trade.

99   Central High Street is shown with St. Lawrence Church left and next to it the Empire Electric Cinema, the first purpose-built cinema in the city. It opened on 18th August 1910 and continued until 1937. Showings took place twice daily at 3 p.m. and 10.30 p.m. with seats priced at 3d, 6d, and 1/-. Picture houses were to proliferate and the company eventually found it could not adapt and was forced to close. A feature seen above the pay box was a globe that stated: 'You know one half of the world, we show you the other.'

EXETER, HIGH STREET

100 Upper High Street had a number of notable buildings including the three-storeyed General Post Office that opened in 1883. It is shown central right with three large Gothic arches. Normal working hours were 7 a.m. to 10 p.m. on every week day. For telegraph business the office was always open. Beyond the Post Office was the entrance to the East Gate Arcade.

HIGH STREET, SHOWING G.P.O. EXETER.

S. A. CHANDLER'S
REAL PHOTO SERIES

101 With the post-war rebuilding of central Exeter street layouts were, in some cases, altered. In this postcard the original corner of the old Paris Street is shown. It extended from Sidwell Street to the Triangle in Newtown, where it joined with Russell Street. Old Paris Street was severely damaged in the Second World War. The Savoy Cinema, shown right, was constructed on the site of the New London Hotel and opened on 22nd November 1936. It proved to be a popular venue, however, in 1972 the building was transformed into a bingo hall and in June 1987 it was demolished to allow for redevelopment.

HIGH STREET, EXETER

L 8533

102 The area of the London Inn Square, pre-war, was a popular meeting place and often used for city events. The immediate location included one of Exeter's finest hotels, a cinema, a range of good shops and of course the East Gate Arcade. Outside the shop Maison de Modes at 271 High Street a group of ladies have set up some stalls selling flowers, fruit and plants. The gentleman with the peaked cap may have been associated with the Plaza Cinema.

103   Pre-war Paris Street was much narrower than its modern replacement and its layout changed after the war. On the left is seen the Elim Tabernacle Church that survived the ravages of war, but only to be demolished after. Opposite the church was the Queens Hall that was transformed into the Palladium Cinema in 1921. The building provided seating for 800 people and was owned by Gaumont British Ltd. up until 1940. It was used as a store until 1942 when it was destroyed in the blitz.

104 The construction of Dix's Field in the early 19th century provided highly desirable living accommodation and it is seen here from the entrance in Southernhay East. Over a period of time the buildings were to be used for offices and the YWCA took up residence in 1906. The residents could take their ease in a communal garden that was railed. Badly damaged during the last war a section of the east side remained but was removed to allow the building of the Civic Centre.

105 A rare image shows the south end of Dix's Field looking towards Southernhay. The central garden is clearly shown and the spire of Southernhay Congregational Church stands at the entrance.

Dix's Field, Exeter.

106   This photograph shows, what might be, the only record of the interior of the Harry Hems workshops in Longbrook Street. The studio, built in Gothic style in 1881, still bears the sculptor's lucky horseshoe integrated into the design of the building's frontage. Harry Hems, a prolific sculptor, also employed a large number of sculptors and carvers to work at his extensive site. All manner of works were undertaken including an exact copy of the Speaker's Chair from the House of Commons. It was commissioned for the Canadian Parliament. Harry Hems came to Exeter in 1866 and died in 1916 after creating one of the most famous ecclesiastical workshops in the country.

107 Sidwell Street, a busy thoroughfare, pre-war, is shown with two trams heading for High Street. A tramline is shown curving to the right passing into the narrow entrance of Paris Street. The corner of the Bude Hotel is just seen. On the left a horse-drawn coach stands outside the White Lion Hotel, a popular small establishment. Some fine late-19th-century buildings stood adjacent to the hotel that was latterly occupied by Standfield and White Motor Engineers.

108   One of Exeter's finest historical timber doors was used as an advert for a car hire company in Sidwell Street. The fine studded oak door (about 1650) was seen at Adelaide Court, almost opposite St. Sidwell's Church and was one of a number of impressive doors that existed in the city. Exeter Museum records indicate that before the war it was 'in a poor state of repair and should have been removed'.

109 The character of Sidwell Street had developed over a long period of time and this was reflected in the variety of buildings and businesses found in the street. A top hatted driver is seen quietly bringing his carriage down the street and passing under a tram traction pole. A number of interesting properties existed in the street right up to the 1960s but were removed in the name of progress.

Sidwell St Exeter.

110 In upper Sidwell Street tram traction poles were centrally placed and two lines operated. On the far right are seen the double fronted premises used as a branch of Lloyds Bank. Buildings in this section of the street, numbers 71 to 79, were to be removed for the building of the Odeon Cinema in 1936. The cinema opened on 30th August 1937.

111 The junction of Sidwell Street, Blackboy Road and Old Tiverton Road is shown in 1887 with two decorated celebration arches crossing the street. They were erected for Queen Victoria's Jubilee. Inscribed on the arches was the declaration 'Her throne unshaken still broad based upon the peoples will'. In the centre of the photograph is the horse trough dedicated in 1879 to the Exeter Surgeon Arthur Kempe, it was known as 'Kempe's Drinking Fountain'.

112 Fore Street is shown around 1910 with a tram negotiating the steep incline. St. John's Church is shown with its bracket clock. The Ironmonger 'Newcombe's' is next door. A bowler hatted man stands with a handcart that contains household items held together with rope. He stands outside 'Gales the Grocers' whose frontage displays a fine gas lamp.

113   The arrival of electric trams in Exeter in 1905 was a time for great celebration and the streets were decked with flags and bunting. This view, taken near the top of Fore Street, shows the new tram lines and horse-drawn vehicles. A large flag flutters from the top of Lloyds Cigarette Factory and also from the tower of St. Petrock's Church. Numerous flagpoles project out over the street.

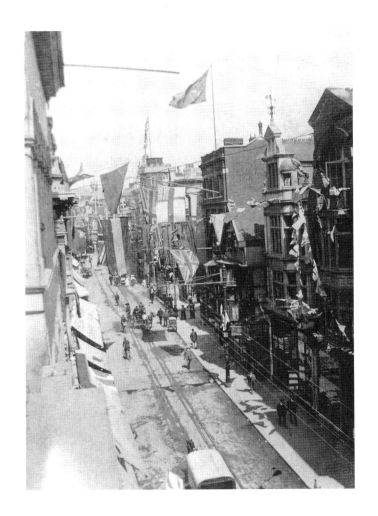

114 Fore Street is shown at its central section with St. John's Church right. Adjacent to it is Number 110 Fore Street, the premises of Walter Otton Ironmongers. The company was a leading supplier of sheet and bar iron and steel and was a prominent wholesaler in the area. An extensive stock of ironmongery was held at this property and also 135 Fore Street. Otton's held the sole agency for Lancashire Patent Belting that was unaffected by water, heat, steam or acids and had a wide range of applications for running machinery.

115   Fore Street was renowned for the variety of trades that operated in the street. The south side would catch the full effect of the afternoon sun, so shop blinds were often a necessity. This photograph from the Chandler Real Photo Series shows road works taking place without any protective barriers. A risky procedure as the steepness of the street often led to serious accidents with runaway vehicles or horses out of control. The Devonport Inn is shown left.

Fore Street, Exeter.

116 St. Mary Steps Church and West Street is shown looking towards Fore Street. To the right the horse-drawn cart appears to have steam coming out of the cart and to the left is seen what may be the only record of a horse-drawn dustcart. An early motor-cycle and sidecar pass by (centre). The buildings shown right are boarded up on the ground floor with a small entrance.

117 West Street takes its name from the ancient West Gate demolished in 1815. Part of the city wall was retained that backed onto an early building on the corner of West Street. The building was probably from the 15th or 16th century but was removed in 1941. It had been partly extended. The site was left empty for a period of twenty years. To the left is seen one of Exeter's older streets, Rack Close Lane that ran along the outside of the city wall and had an open gutter.

118 From the 15th to 18th centuries Exeter's West Quarter was inhabited by merchants whose business revolved around trading and shipping. Prestigious timber framed buildings were constructed and a number of these survived right up until the 1930s. Sixteenth-century properties at the bottom of Stepcote Hill, seen here in poor condition were to be saved and restored after a campaign for their retention. A sign on the building states 'E. Willis best prices quoted for rags, bones and bottles'.

119　A fascinating social scene is captured in West Street against a backdrop of some of Exeter's oldest buildings. The three buildings shown right no longer exist but at this time were occupied by E. Pearse & Co, Rag, Bone and Skin Merchants. The property seen left, at the bottom of Stepcote Hill, has S. Cridland written on its frontage. Children are playing in the street and a large horse-drawn cart carrying a large quantity of wicker baskets is being attended to by a lady in a long dress, much to the interest of onlookers.

West Street & Old Houses, Exeter.

120　For the visitor entering Exeter through the West Gate in times gone by this postcard gives an idea of what they may have seen. The remains of the City Wall are seen left with an early property abutting it. St. Mary Steps Church stands beside Stepcote Hill and is flanked by two fine 16th-century timber framed buildings. The hill leads directly up to the city centre. It was from this site that William of Orange entered Exeter with his army in 1688.

121   In Victorian times Mission Work in the West Quarter was an important factor in helping to maintain the community. Farthing breakfasts were instigated and distributed from Ewings Lane off West Street. In the late 19th century a purpose-built Mission Hall was constructed on Exe Island and fronted by buildings with an arched entrance off the street. It also had a unique covered tunnel entrance from a third storey in New Bridge Street directly into its first floor. The buildings in Exe Island were demolished in the early 1960s to facilitate a new entrance to Exe Island and the creation of Western Way Inner Bypass, but the Mission Hall remains.

122 Tudor Street, part of Exe Island, had a number of interesting buildings, but its most noted was to become known as 'The Tudor House'. Dating from 1630 the property had become derelict and in 1963 was purchased by local restorer Bill Lovell, who took twelve years to restore it. All appropriately aged materials were used and undertaken in the manner of when it was first built. After its restoration the building was sold. Our record shows the property with is unusual slate front bearing coats of arms of the original owners.

123   In 1927 an extraordinary event took place when the City Wall fell on the Custom House Inn that stood at the bottom of Quay Hill. The public house extended around the corner of the wall at the bottom of Quay Lane and the collapse, together with a slight landslide, destroyed the property. Following this event investigations took place and building within certain distances of the ancient fabric was regulated. The photograph taken from the City Wall looks down on Quay Lane and shows the once narrow Horse Lane that led from the Friars to the Quay.

124 Leaving the City centre and heading for Topsham the route follows South Street, Holloway Street and Topsham Road. The hill leading from Holloway Street is the start of Topsham Road and Number 1 Topsham Road is shown left in this photo of about 1910. The steep hill leads to St. Leonard's Church and what was known as St. Leonard's Down. At the top of the hill was a pedestrian bridge built for the Baring family, owners of Mount Radford House, to attend church. The simple ironwork bridge and brick arch were removed in the 1930s. A culverted brook still flows down through the valley to the river and under the road the early medieval bridge survives.